# A Journey to the Sacred Shore

## Roz Winters

*Can you feel the age of your Soul?*

*Can you sense your heart's journey?*

*There is a deeper life that
you are living,*

*for the Soul is an ancient traveller.*

*How many know their Soul's story?*

First published in Australia in 2011 by

MBS Press (Mind Body Spirit)
A division of Pick-a-WooWoo Publishers
Nannup, Western Australia 6275
**Copyright © 2011**

The moral right of Roz Winters to be identified as the Author has been asserted by her in accordance with the Copyright, Designs and Patents Act 1988. All rights reserved. No part of this book may be used or reproduced, stored in a retrieval system, or transmitted in any form, or by any means electronic, mechanical, recording, photocopying, or in any manner whatsoever without permission in writing from the publisher, except for book reviews.

**National Library of Australia Cataloguing-in-Publication entry**
Author: Winters, Roz.
Title: A journey to the sacred shore/ Roz Winters.
ISBN: 9781921883200 (pbk.)
Dewey Number: A823.4

**Publishing Details**
Published in Australia – MBS Press (Mind Body Spirit)
(A division of Pick-A-Woo Woo Publishers)

**Printed through Lightning Source (USA/UK/AUS)**
Available via:

**United States**
Ingram Book Company; Amazon.com; Baker & Taylor

**Canada**
Chapters Indigo; Amazon Canada

**United Kingdom**
Amazon.com; Bertrams; Book Depository Ltd; Gardners; Mallory International

**Australia**
DA Information Services; The Nile; Emporium Books Online; James Bennet (Australian Libraries) Dennis Jones and Associates; Brumby Books and Music
www.mbspress.com

The Author can be contacted through her website
http://www.otherworldmusic.com

# Contents

The Soul introduces herself .................................................................. iv

Part 1 - Come with me on a journey to the Soul's sacred shore ....... 1

Part 2 - We visit the Soul in her own realm ..................................... 11

Part 3 - The path leads into the forest ................................................ 25

Part 4 - We meet the eternal feminine spirit within us all ................ 45

Part 5 - Renewal…healing ourselves…and the Earth ..................... 63

Part 6 - The path leads back to the hearth ......................................... 77

Part 7 - …And into the Light… ......................................................... 89

Pathways that lead to the sacred shore…......................................... 106

Notes .................................................................................................. 108

Acknowledgements ........................................................................... 109

# *The Soul introduces herself*

My home is in the soft white ethers that permeate the universe, where I dance with feather-light steps around all living things. My purpose is to awaken you to spirit, but first you must invite me into your life. Love is the path that leads directly to me.

I am asleep in those who live only for material things, and I do not exist for those who cause suffering in their world. Yet the path of tears also leads to my sacred shore of peace, because all paths lead to me.

Finding me will take you beyond your biology, to the Soul-light that shines like a beacon in the darkness of the world. My Light will reveal to you the link between all living things, and the truth that what you do to another - you also do to yourself.

In a Yang-dominated world I bring Yin. In a cold universe I bring Quintessence. I am the dark matter of mystery and the key to all puzzles.

I am the Soul.

I am often personified as a feminine being, but really there is no gender in my world. My beautiful wings wrap around all living things.

Those who use their Soul light as a lamp for others - are the gatherers of life whose invisible arms hold the world together.

I am powerful in my own realm but delicate in the world of gravity, so you may only approach me with your most gentle heart. Look for me also in the eyes of those who mirror your own true face.

The forests of Gaia reflect my otherworld forests, where you can always attune to me through Nature and her sacred places.

I am what is missing in the world.... and what you are searching for.

Walk with me now to the sacred shore…

I am the Soul.

# Part 1

# *Come with me on a journey to the Soul's sacred shore*

## Finding the way

There are many names for our spiritual home – Heaven, Nirvana, Shangri-la, and the Otherworld, are some of the names used by the ancients to describe the gateway to other realms. It is the land where poets and those of gentle heart feel most at home. The ancient Celts called this place Hy Brasil, the land to the west. Sailors often searched for this mysterious land, that was in fact not a physical place at all, but one of the great Soul lands.

From the perspective of the human journey, within the realm of Time, the Soul has wandered for eons through ancestral woods, searching for Home. In today's world the search is no different, as we wander through the labyrinths of city life.

Every culture has stories to tell about the journey of the Soul, and above the differences in language, culture and creed, they have a common belief – that the human race is One family within the diversity of life on Earth.

It was the birds that called me to the heavenly lands. They crowded my garden and led me in sleep, to the land of Silver Palms. They taught me how to use my singing to bring peace to troubled hearts. I met the angels of Nature, who act as guiding and balancing forces within the great body of the Earth. We journey through the forest of life as if looking for something lost. We approach the world with action, whereas the inner world is found through stillness.

The sacred shore awaits you…

## We enter the otherworld forest of Broceliande

Time is slow in the twilight wood, where vegetation takes its time.
Nature never hurries; she has her own pace,
while saving us from ourselves.
Do you see life changing on Gaia's surface with the clearing of trees and birds disappearing?
See how the climate moves…
Greed has won the day, but it is never too late to change.

Deep in the forest of Broceliande the traveller wanders,
through ancient pine and leafy grove,
searching for Home.

Unexpectedly one may come across this land…
Pilgrims were often unaware of where they were, until they left, and the way was closed…

The ancients were afraid of the land where dragons dwell, and ignored the Fae folk who lived there, unaware that they had pierced the veil between the worlds. In time they realised that the Fae were otherworldly beings, and left them in peace.

Journey to the sacred shore of Being where the way is clear and the heart sings out in joy. The way to Broceliande is through the Heart – the only true compass.

Enchanted waters and dancing trees welcome the traveller.
Mistletoe and leaping salmon are signs that the otherworld
is near.
You will hear the song of falling leaves,
the deep hum of the soil and movement of the devas.
Where waters murmur and stones whisper…

You may be walking quietly through a garden or woodland,
when the atmosphere slowly changes all around you.
The birds stop singing, as if Nature has paused.
There is a silence…like mist descending.
Slowly Gaia's secret door opens,
and her arms reach out to the seeker.
When you approach the majesty of Nature with respect,
she will sing to you her sweetest songs.

Journey to the sacred shore.
Why waste time! Follow the path of Soul,
far away from noise and bustling life,
and into Gaia's fond embrace.

Earthchild arrived in Broceliande
carrying her burden of life.
She lay wearily beneath a large Oak tree and closed her eyes
to rest, when she felt a pulse not her own…
It was a Dryad moving through the tree to comfort her.
A branch reached down and touched her cheek,
like angels do when we are sad.
Earthchild felt the beating heart of the tree,
and her sadness disappeared.

Journey to the sacred shore where peaceful swans glide
over the lake.
Sometimes the Soul moves like a winged creature longing
for Home…
Contemplation of the heart will lead the way
to the land of Eternal Light.

Iona's shores are awash with mist…the little white isle that
St Columba made his home long ago.
Iona is one of Gaia's sacred shores, where the power of Spirit
is strong.
Wavelets gently lap in the eye of the moon.
Seagulls call as they fly over her pure white sands.
Iona's lamp burns brightly, drawing pilgrims to her shore of
peace, attracted by her light of Hope
and her prayers of Peace.
When you sit at Gaia's feet and pay homage to her,
she will answer your deepest prayers.
The gateway is through the Soul light within.

What is the prayer of the seeker?
What are the three signs that Home is near?
Joy – the lightness of a Soul awakened.
Heart – when compassion lights the way in your life.
Belonging – finding your true Home.
Deeper goes the traveller into the night.
The Soul is a tracker through the forest of Becoming.
By night she is an owl;
by day a butterfly.
Journey to the sacred shore of Being.

Feel the spiritual sun deep inside and rekindle your dreams.
The sunspirit shines more brightly than the Sun!
Shine your being out into the world.
Weaving through bushes, slipping past flowers…
contentment will come.

Gaia is on loan to the dwellers on her surface.
Those who are anchored on the sacred shore will not harm even the smallest living thing.
Is this not the way to peace?

Listen to the voice of the otherworld messenger,
who tells us,
'Our world is real, more so than yours.
How can yours be real when everything dies.
Nothing dies here, because it is real.
Your world is a reflection, a dream within a dream.
Look beyond your world, we are not far;
only a breath away'.

'Listen, you may hear us…
Look out of the corner of your eye…you may see us.'

Find peace and take it into your world.
Your life is precious.
Find your way home, don't waste time.
The peaceful swans are circling the lake.
Journey to the sacred shore and find rest…

# *The Soul speaks*

I am a spark of light in your world.
Sometimes you may catch a glimpse of me
on Gaia's shores.

*A new day is dawning...*

# Part 2

# We visit the Soul in her own realm

## The Soul nourishes us

The Soul lives and breathes in invisible space, and nourishes us with the food of spirit. Without Soul contact we live in spiritual famine, for it is she who carries us through the darkest nights. The Soul is not subject to earthly existence, yet she permeates our being once we ascend to our awakened life. In fact, she is always with us, but the great sleep keeps us from reaching her light.

The Soul is fragile, yet powerful in her own realm. Think of the power that holds the universe together, mixed with the finest weaving of a petal, and then you will know the magic of the Soul.

Sensing her presence is a radiant moment of awakening. Her light brings inner wisdom, and the dawning of the astounding truth that heaven is *now*; that everything is right here, right now. She is the beautiful angel that unites us in Oneness with all things. When her light descends on us, a light also ascends from us, to meet her in unity. This is how we bring heaven down to Earth.

So what is this slumber that keeps us from experiencing our Soul life? It is the wavering emotions that constantly wash over us, like clouds blocking the Sun. It is our busy lives that overtake the inner silence; a lovely silence that exists deep within us at all times.

The Soul is beyond all pain, yet it is often suffering that leads us to her gate.

On a twilight moon, circled in a fragile mist, the Soul calls us with her song –

>I am a golden bridge in Time
>A winged being
>unseen
>yet existing
>Hear my voice calling you
>
>Come and build your golden bridge with me
>I am waiting for you
>Rise above earthly cares and
>reach out and touch my hand
>
>I am as close to you as a whisper
>I am right here…

## *The Soul speaks*

Noise drowns my song
and materialism masks my existence.
Rise above the layers of life
And re-unite with me.

## *Her garden is filled with flowers*

Close your eyes and follow the gentle path that leads to the rose garden of the Soul. In the centre of this inner garden, visualise a willow tree. Sit quietly beneath her green soft shade and you will hear her whispering songs to the sky. The birds are always respectfully silent when listening to the ancient songs of the trees:

> I soothe the heart of those
> who sit beneath my waving fronds.
> My body is a shelter
> for all Gaia's creatures.

In the rose garden the delicate gossamer layers of life just float away, to reveal the pure diamond that you are. As your true self is uncovered, you will wonder why you never felt the secret layers of the false self settle upon you over the years.

The body is your vehicle on Earth, growing and ageing through time, but the Soul does not age, and touching Soul is touching your immortality, your true Self. The Soul can move between worlds, especially in utero, and babies who die before birth, are safely transported back to the Soul fields of bliss, unaffected by their brief earthly journey.

The Soul may take you travelling through invisible space to the many levels of existence beyond our third dimensional life. Science is already pondering these ancient truths. Being alive is an opportunity, and you are a powerhouse of energy with a unique destiny.

Humans have always searched for a paradise on Earth. The Alchemists worked tirelessly to turn base metal into gold. King Arthur searched for the Holy Grail. Yet what they searched for was already within their hearts – the gold of their own eternal Being.

There are sacred places on Earth that are conducive to Soul travel, and being there may help you find the way. Santorini in Greece and the Isle of Iona in Scotland, are two places that hold the Soul light so well. Gaia often gives pointers and clues to her higher origins, for she too is on her own spiritual journey.

The rose garden blossoms in the love you feel for your children, for the orphans or helpless ones. Whenever your heart reaches out, you are in the garden of spirit. You may wonder just how to begin, but by reading these words, you already have! When the Soul takes charge, your life will open to signs and synchronicities that will guide you Home.

Find peace and bask in your own radiant wisdom.

The sacred shore is only a breath away.

## *A precious life*

There is another life that you are living;
a deeper life of spirit that is alive in you.
It *is* you.
It is a life more beautiful than all the beauty on earth, permanent, undying.
Can you sense the journey?
Life is like a mirage…an image in a mirror;
a dream within a dream.
Yet here you are, living in a universe of galaxies birthing and dying;
following the rules of physical existence.
Look beyond these cycles of change and come into my world.

So how do you find this deeper life?
There are signs and clues in the labyrinth of life.
In quiet contemplation your awareness will rise.
Watch the swans as they glide upon a peaceful lake.
Honour the majesty of the Silent Hill.
Peace will begin to grow in your heart.
Live this precious life, but know that there is so much more…

## *The Soul speaks*

Relax on my sacred shore
and listen to my harmonies of light.

## Approaching the gateway

There are worlds beyond our own that overlap each other in consistent waves, dancing together in a harmony of sound and enfoldment. Earth is but one of these worlds.

For centuries mystics have described the many dimensions that exist beyond the worlds shown to us through the lenses in our eyes. Physicists are now suggesting that our world is a projection from a level of reality beyond space and time.

Here on Earth there are beings that live in the wind – billowing, rising and surfing the breeze. Some are like whirling dervishes who spin like tops, using the sky as their dance floor. Beings exist within the flame and soil that are part of the building blocks of the moving universe.

All spiritual paths eventually lead to the understanding of the Oneness of all things. The ancient mysteries and great books of truth will guide you. It is hoped that this book will whet your appetite to find out more. Whether it is Vedic poetry, Buddhism, the Koran, Kabala, Gnosticism or the Bible, they all lead to the Divine Gateway, where all is One. We are all brothers and sisters on a path that leads us Home. You can find the way without books or doctrines, for the truth also exists within your heart.

How exquisite is the Divine as it manifests through its creation…

## Music of the spheres

Beautiful music will open the gate to the Soul realm, transporting you to the land of Heart's Desire. Music reaches deep inside the Soul in a way that words cannot. There are no strangers when people come together in music, where all sounds commune as one without the burden of language.

Music is everywhere, from the human voice to nature's cascading waters and green landscapes. Bells with a sweet tone have been known to take the traveller beyond Earthly shores to the land of Bliss. Wooden instruments will transport the listener to the sacred shore if the Dryad is still living within the wood. The best violins are made by luthiers who revere the spiritual beauty of trees, and carefully carve their instruments without evicting the Dryad from its home.

Nature's music is heard within all her elements – in the crackle of flames or wind through the trees. Soil and stone have their melody and crystals hum their own refrain. Grass and flowers sound the harmony, while trees chant the universal rhythms.

Birds are the great carriers of beautiful music. In Celtic stories the faeries often shape shift into birds to bring music to the human world. Some say Heaven itself continuously plays beautiful music.

Sound is an important part of bringing forth the Aquarian age. Each sign of the zodiac rules a particular part of the body. Generally Aries rules the head, and Taurus rules the throat. The signs then descend to the last sign of Pisces which rules the feet. When awakening occurs, the signs are reversed, and Aries rules the feet, ascending to Pisces at the crown chakra, and Aquarius ruling the throat.

Become a channel for peace in the world by bringing radiant music into your life…

## *Love is all you need*

There is a Great Love that moves the universe and calls us into life. It is the burst of creation from the womb of eternal existence. The Great Love includes everything, from an inchworm to the birth of galaxies. When personified, it is the force that some call their God/dess; yet the Great Love need not be worshipped as something external, for it exists within us all.

On the summit of Mount Everest it is there. In a drop of water, it is there. Whether or not we can feel the Great Love, it is there.

When you find this love within your heart, there is no longer a need for spiritual laws, for the Great Love is beyond all human doctrines. So much time is spent searching for someone to be that Great Love; but whether someone loves you or not, the Great Love is there within you…loving you. The Soul will be your guide:

> You are in the house of the Beloved
> Look out the window – I am there
> Open the door – I am there
> Every path leads to me
> Every gate opens to me
> By the hearth – I am there
> Every flame dances to me
> There is no need to worry at all…

## *The Soul speaks*

You will find me in the silent and pure arms
of nature's forests.

*Part 3*

*The path leads into the forest*

# The forest as Soul

> *Viriditas (green power) is God's creative power manifest in the created world of nature.*
> Hildegarde von Bingen

The forest is a metaphor for the Soul, and when spiritual values disappear, so do the forests. A walk through nature's woodlands will bring you in close contact with life in its pure form, where there is medicine for the body and peace for the mind. Sit in the lush greenness of the forest and you will sense her vibrant life force all around you. Trees, plants and stones are all part of the forest, and there is no better place to sense the connection with all living things. Losing touch with nature ungrounds us, and the illusion of separation creates a lifeless world where we ignore the stranger; where my harp is just a piece of wood with strings attached. In oneness, my harp and I resonate together in a vibrating musical universe, where there are no strangers in the dancing movement of life. Each sense has its own way of recognising sacredness, from the fragrance of flowers to the sweetest tasting food. This is why children love sweet foods so much, because it reminds them of their prenatal existence in the pure land of Soul.

The indigenous cultures of the world are Gaia's gatekeepers. They sing her songs, dance her history, and listen to the ancient voices of forest, ocean and desert. They hold the key to Gaia's health and healing…

## *There is a tree that grows within*

There is a tree that grows within your heart, with fine white blossoms and deep green leaves. The roots grow down beneath your feet, anchoring you on Gaia's shores. Her branching leafy hair flows up toward the heavens, as she slowly sways in the gentle breeze.

The tree that grows within your heart will guide you through the changes in your life. Visualise her, for this is where your true self is born – upon her firm branches; safe among her green foliage.

Once you commune with the tree that grows within your heart, you will understand why forests must be saved. They are part of the great body of Gaia.

She also grows fine white blossoms.

She too has a heart.

## *The Soul speaks*

The beauty of a sunset
or the joy of a forgiving heart,
will open the door to my world.

# The story of trees

*The trees are singing my music. Or have I sung theirs?*
Edward Elgar

Forests are still disappearing at an alarming rate, but the world is waking up to the wonder of trees. Trees have existed on Earth longer than animals and humans. The root system of a tree is a masterpiece of nature and acts as a storage bank for carbon dioxide, one of the greenhouse gases. Fossil fuels come from tree and plant fossils from the Carboniferous period of 300 million years ago. Nothing is wasted on Gaia's vast body, with ancestral trees fuelling our lives today. The end of fossil fuel is near and a dynasty will close, but a more beautiful one will arise with cleaner forms of energy.
Gaia tells us –

> Be mindful as you walk on my body.
> Step gently and feel my heart beating beneath
> your feet.
> Sit with me and tell me your story,
> then I will tell you mine.

Trees bring strength to the land, preventing landslides and retaining water for the surrounding soil. A 30 foot tree may have roots that extend horizontally for up to 90 feet out from the trunk. The world's tallest tree is a 367 foot high Redwood in the U.S.A. The tallest tree ever recorded was in Victoria, Australia, but was cut down last century.

There is no lovelier experience that communing with a tree. Children do it quite naturally, and stroke trees as if they are friendly animals. When we commune with something, we become it, and there is an empathic exchange of energy. Once you have communed with a tree your life will change forever, because you will be awakened to the world of energy, where all life is united as one. You will never again doubt that trees have some form of awareness and that they can reach out to other life forms and communicate with them. There are many stories of tree communication, from trees consoling people who are grieving, to happy communions with groups of young trees.

In his book *Man's Search for Meaning*, Viktor Frankl tells the story of a young woman he met in the concentration camps during the Second World War. She was seriously ill, and he asked her how she stayed so cheerful. She told him about a little tree outside her window that she talked to in her loneliness. Upon asking if the tree ever replied, she said 'Yes, it says *I am here, I am here, I am life, eternal life.*'

Tree lovers everywhere sense the distress of a tree being cut down. Tree hugging is a growing response to the senseless destruction of trees, and the Chipko[2] movement in India led the way by asking people to go out and hug the oldest living beings on Earth. The ancient cultures see trees as a symbol of body and spirit, with branches reaching to the sky and roots firmly planted on the earth. This symbolic world tree stood in the centre of all life, passing through the three cosmic zones – underworld, earth and sky. Trees are the spine of Gaia; the strength and support for us all. The spirit of the tree sings,

I live deep in the Earth,
yet sway with the sun in the sky.
I am the bridge between the worlds,
I grow with the power of the land.
Here my voice calling you to come back
to your Soul.

Buddha was enlightened beneath a tree and the Norse god Odin hung on the world tree – Yggdrasil[3] – and received spiritual wisdom for his people in the form of the runes. Druids are the Celtic keeper of the trees and believed that humans originated from trees. When a Druid died, a special tree would be hollowed out and his body placed inside, thus returning him to the source. This is how coffins originated.

In his *Interview with a Yew Tree*, the Druid Greywolf asks the Yew, 'What is your wyrd (fate)?' The Yew replies, 'The wyrd of all living things – beauty then death.'

Some say that when a tree is cut down its spirit dies, but the 6th century Welsh Druid Taliesin assured us that the spirit remains if the wood is made into a wand or a musical instrument. If a tree dies naturally then the spirit of the tree will not be harmed. Sit quietly beneath a beloved tree and you may feel its heartbeat. In silence and peace the tree will commune with you.

## *Norfolk Pine speaks*

In stillness, we hold the land together
with roots that grip and secure Gaia's shores.
In movement, you are the builders
helping life forms to thrive on Gaia's land.
Gaia cannot survive without her trees.
Trees personify the stately power of the universe.

## *The Soul touches Gaia in her wilder-land*

The power of the forest rises up through us, with a fragrance that melts into our body, nourishing the life force within. Elemental powers stir the heart to heal itself, for the forest is a place of solace and rest.

Forests have existed longer than humans and most animals. Life was birthed into the arms of Gaia with everything needed to survive. From the deep green forests of Caledon, to the magical rainforests on Gaia's tropical belt, our ancestors thrived and grew from the potency and pulse of the land.

Once you relax in shaded woodland, you are hypnotised by the aromas that weave around your senses. When Gaia opens her secret door, you will see the world through the eyes of nature. The character of a tree can be seen by its shape, and have been known to commune with passers by. One afternoon while walking through the forest of Huelgoat in France, I was overwhelmed by the smell of roses, though there were none nearby. I realised that the elementals were communing with me by releasing their perfume!

The ancient Druids built their temples in the forests and were perhaps the first temples ever built on Earth. Druid priests and priestesses entered these temples, or Nemetoi, where they performed rituals to the Sun and universal forces. All trees are sacred to the Druids, but most revered is the Oak tree. The ancient word for Oak was *duir,* and where the word *door* comes from. Druids regard the Oak as a doorway to the otherworld and the ancestors. The Oak is most sacred when

Mistletoe is growing on its branches. Mistletoe represents male fertility and is offered to the Goddess Gaia, where the union of male and female energy promises the growth of nature and new life. The woodlands offer deep healing for those who seek respite from their busy lives.

The loss of Soul values in the world links directly with the destruction of forests. Without forests we are left with a barren wasteland, and without Soul contact we are spiritually empty. The Soul is often visualized in meditation as a beautiful place, perhaps a garden or clearing in a forest. It may be an ethereal place of light or a tropical island. Cultivation of Soul contact is vital for the journey through life, and the Soul guides you on your passage to the spirit lands when you leave Gaia's shores. When the Soul light is awakened, you become a beacon for others, who will bathe in your Light.

The forest also represents our inner wilder-ness – the natural state that we can lose sight of in our 'civilised' society. It is the place where we can be grounded and natural, without glamour or pretense. Many young people today act out the rituals of ancient tribal cultures, as can be seen in the mosh pits of modern rock music, where they release the rajasic forces of fire and movement. The Soul is always free and Soul contact brings all truth into the light. It is never too late to come home to the forest within your Soul.

## We stop to rest in the Green Chapel...

The green light of the forest holds the key to peace. Come with me on a journey to the forest of Soul:

Visualise yourself sitting on a large rock in a beautiful green forest, surrounded by moss-covered stones and tall trees. The Sun is overhead. Nature welcomes you to her Green Chapel, where plants whisper their quiet poetry and trees open their eyes to you. Nature has gathered here for you.

The forest is lit with bright green splendour as the Sun wanders slowly across the sky, playing hide and seek between the treetops. In the distance is the sound of small chirping birds. A trickle of water can be heard, and a small stream bubbles and skips over pebbles of all shapes and sizes. The water divides into streamlets that spread out across the land, only to meet again as they pass by the rock that you are sitting on. The streamlets gather in a communion of water, and drop over the edge of a small rock face worn by time. The gentle cascade becomes a tiny waterfall, and surrounding trees soak their roots while small creatures swim in the dancing waters.

Bathe in this image while the green wisdom of the forest nourishes your Soul, allowing the gentle waters to flow through the parched areas of your life, to feed your spirit.

You are now communing with the spirit of the Earth and *all* of nature. Feel the beauty and silence of her powerful, yet fragile body, and send love to the great mother Gaia who gave birth to us all. Feel her large arms reaching out to embrace you, and send love to her in return. Love sent out to others is always returned to you.

You are One with nature and nature is One with you.

All is as it should be.

All time is now.

You are blessed.

The spirit of the Earth will stay with you forever.

## We meet the builders of form

Elementals are the great builders of form on the Earth. Their movement can be felt everywhere, but they are more likely to show themselves to humans in forests and green lands. Every element has its own angel; even concrete and plastic are a part of the great oneness of life, for everything is born from the body of Gaia.

In the 15th century, Paracelsus called these four forces of nature elementals – the Gnomes of earth, Sylphs of air, Salamanders or fire and Undines of water. These forces are often personified in human form as the little people who push the flowers through the soil, or the winged beings who move the winds. Some see elementals as orbs of light, floating or pulsing with colour.

Sylphs can be seen surfing the airways on windy days, moving quickly with ethereal wispy bodies. I have seen a great Deva of the air hovering high over the sea, floating in layers of chiffon with huge wings that span the sky. Devas are beings that watch over vast areas of land or sea. Every country has its own Deva, and Gaia also has her own luminous Devic protector.

The best place to see the elementals at work is in the silence of nature. But even in the city they can be seen wherever there are growing things. My little dog was startled when she was pushed out of the way by an invisible hand (or foot!), when she went close to a tree on our daily walk.

One need only sit by a fireside or bonfire for a few seconds to become aware of the Salamanders of fire. They are not as friendly as the other elementals, and you can only watch in awe as they perform their crazy dance of freedom within the flames. The tribal/trance dances that are so popular in dance halls today are similar to the crazy dance of the Salamanders.

The Undines are water spirits who may be seen in the movement of all water. For centuries sailors have sighted Undines in the form of mermaids. In still water we can see our reflection, but if you look closely you may in fact see the face of an Undine beneath the ripples. Many photographs have been taken of Undines swimming just below the surface of lakes and ponds.

Gnomes are the earth spirits and keepers of stone, rock and soil. They can be very cheeky and are always busy, much like children, whom they love. Gnomes are known to be accident prone, so if you hear a loud noise in your garden, it may be a Gnome tripping over something. So much for being elusive!

Within the earth element are the beautiful nature spirits known as Dryads. The Dryad is the spirit of the tree, and can move from tree to tree without being seen, by moving through branches and roots that connect under the soil. This is known as forest walking. For those lucky enough to meet a Dryad, they have much knowledge to impart about the green life of nature.

In the ancient Greek story, Rhoecus finds out what happens when you harm any living thing. The little Dryad tells him, 'One who scorns even the smallest thing alive is forever shut away from all that is beautiful in nature.'

There is a lovely story about an elderly Scottish man who met a Faun in Edinburgh's Botanic Gardens in the 1960s. Mr. R. Ogilvie Crombie, affectionately known as Roc, published a book about his encounter with the little Faun, and the message he gave was about the survival of the planet itself. He told Roc that humans need to regain their respect and love for nature before it is too late.

Humans spend time watching nature, but nature is also watching us…

## *The Soul speaks*

My journey is beyond time and space,
Yet I live and move within your heart.

## *Earthchild's journey*

Earthchild[4] travels into the forest looking for her way.
She communes with trees, plants and stones
in their world of Sacred Green.
She greets the spirits of nature, who are part of the radiant glory of Earth –
in the trickle of a stream, the sighing of the wind,
and in the roar of mighty oceans.
Tree spirits guide her for they are great and wise beings.
With their help, she finds her way.

Passing by the stream of Quiet Water, Earthchild stops to rest a while.
A whispering sound slowly begins to resonate around her, and the forest becomes a vessel for the sacred sound.
She hears the call of the Devas, whose music awakens the heart and heals all things.
Earthchild closes her eyes to listen, as only truth comes from the heart.
In this way, she finds herself.

Darkness falls and Earthchild lights a candle.
On a journey dangerous at night, she calls on Druantia, a tree spirit, who leads her through the marshes and dark places.
She hers the sound of the night creatures, but her light keeps them away, as nothing can harm the gentle heart.
Morning comes.
Earthchild arrives at the Waterfall of Bliss.
There in the dancing waters she meets the Beloved.

## *A child asked me a profound question*

Four year old Michelle asked me,
'Who pushes the flowers out of the ground and makes the grass grow?'
I told her that this was the work of the angels of nature.
She ran off to play, barefooted on the grass,
but quickly returned to tell me that she could feel the angels in her feet!

Out of the mouth of babes…

# *The Soul speaks*

Contact with me will awaken you
to the Self that is always free.
I am the doorway to all happiness.
Close your eyes and call on me.
I will come.

# Part 4

# We meet the eternal feminine spirit within us all

# The eternal feminine spirit

*The eternal feminine spirit draweth us ever onward.*
Goethe

The eternal feminine spirit has a voice,
She is no longer silent like whispering trees,
She lives in quiet places.
Even amidst the rush of life she will find a peaceful place to be.
Like a leaf in the wind she travels through invisible space, yet she also abides in nature.
She is all-knowing, you cannot fool her,
She is the psychic within us all.
Time does not exist in her world so her patience is endless.
No-one speaks for her, she channels herself,
Her own deep wisdom brings balance to the world.

She is vulnerable to the aggressions of Man.
For so long she has been silenced by the iron word.
For centuries seen only as a plaything with no power of her own. Yet throughout history her spirit endured, for she is the Eternal Flame that gives hope to the world.

As the poet and seer she communicates wisdom, awakening the world to the journey of the Soul.
How many are aware of the path that they have chosen?
A path built even before birth.

The eternal feminine spirit is the divine Goddess,
With millions of altars erected in her name, she may even be a religion in her own right.

The Goddess needs no fanfare to announce her existence, and her devotees are the quiet majority who preach only Love.

The eternal feminine spirit knows that when the world becomes our family, then peace will arise. Only a higher love can transform an uncaring world.

Appearing in many forms her spirit arose – as Sophia, Isis, Mary and our own living Earth – Gaia.
She is the keeper of life.
She is the love of all mothers for their children.
She carries the Light that pierces the darkness.
Those who carry the beauty of life within already know her.

The eternal feminine spirit is the revealer of truth, and only she can silence the God of war.

## *A prophecy is given*

*As our forefathers and elders believed and still believe, the Holy Spirit shall come again which was once mortally born among us as the Son of God, but then shall be the Daughter of God. The Divine Spirit shall come again as a Woman. Then for the first time the world will know Peace.*
Hebridean prophesy

This ancient prophecy from the highlands of Scotland speaks of a second coming. It could be interpreted as the return of the feminine, or awakening of the Soul en masse in the world.

Throughout history the Soul was often personified as a woman, and a favourite is the 15th century Flemish alchemical painting[5] of the Soul personified as a woman, contemplating her heart. In occult literature they speak of the incoming Aquarian age as a 7th ray[6] feminine cycle.

In his book *Return of the Goddess*, Edward Whitmont discusses the new myth rising today, waiting to be integrated into our current worldview. The old ways are dying and a new way is being born. Mythologist Joseph Campbell talked about the 'society of the planet', a new myth that the human race can unite with. He suggested that the symbol for this society could be a photograph of the Earth from space, showing the planet as One World. The awakening of the Soul releases the warmth and protection of the caring feminine spirit, often seen as a haven in her world, whether in woman or man.

There is a feeling of coming home, when the Soul light opens within us. This awakening will take feminine values beyond the home and into the governments of the world, where her caring is needed. The feminine spirit will never accept a world where people are starving and living in desperate conditions. The caring hand of friendship will reach out across the world. This is the promise of a new age.

Feminine values are slowly arising in the world today. There is much work to be done, but nothing can stop the natural balancing laws of the universe.

Behind the outer world of wars and unrest, the eternal feminine spirit of Peace is rising.

## *The Soul speaks*

Sit quietly in the centre of yourself
and you will see all that you need to see.

## Beautiful attractors

All that Gaia produces from her vast body echoes within every living organism, and all life on Earth is an extension of her body. The growth of crystals obeys her 'yin' understanding – the feminine pattern that exists deep within her Soul.

Crystals form when solutions floating within the Earth begin pulling molecules toward it; the 'attracting' force begins forming, binding and growing until a crystal is created. This is the power of the feminine attracting what she needs, so beautifully witnessed in crystal formations.

Gaia is the living crucible where all life transforms and grows from her heat. The spectrum of life on Earth is the result of this fire, with temperatures of up to 500 degrees within the Earth that purify and shape all life. Her fire makes diamonds. In the universal story of creation, life on Earth is a school of learning that transforms us from an uncut gem into a perfect diamond.

For centuries man has mined for gold and diamonds as if they were the Holy Grail. Yet the diamond vessel that he seeks can only be found within his own heart; a diamond that cannot be stolen or destroyed.

When you hold a crystal in your hand you attune to Gaia in a deep way, and your positive thoughts help to balance the effects of the destruction of her green lands.

Gaia is the living cauldron where all things transform and grow from her heart.

## *She carries her own light*

Unlike the moon, the eternal feminine spirit carries her own light within. The moon takes her light from the sun.

Caring for helpless or small creatures will awaken her light within you, for the feminine spirit looks beyond bloodline, and sees all life on earth as one family. This is surely the path to peace.

The eternal feminine spirit shines her caring light onto others, but she must also carry this diffuse light for herself, or she will wither under the scrutiny of the spotlight.

## *The eternal feminine spirit speaks...*

*I am the keeper of the Grail; the one who carries the vessel of Light to the castle of men.*

The eternal feminine spirit awaits you at her silver gates. She travels in the ethers, awakening the hearts of those who call to her. Her temples are scattered across the world – beside rivers, in caves, on altars by the roadside, and in homes everywhere. She lives in the heart of man as well as woman. Her love can be felt in the heart that is open and loving.

Visualise her flame. Her feminine light can be seen in the Moon, and also in candlelight and crystals.

She is the softness of lamplight.
She is the serenity of a beautiful rose quartz.
Her light brings peace to you heart.

Call on the eternal feminine spirit to soothe your world.

Come and sit by her sacred shore of peace.

## The world of the feminine is timeless

The world of the feminine belongs in natural time, beyond clocks and timetables. Her womb spans a universe of planets and stars, giving birth to galaxies at every moment. She was the midwife when Gaia formed her wordless harmony of life. Time is a man-made concept.

Living in natural time brings us closer to the life we lived as children. Do you remember the long summer days and how they seemed to last forever? That is the real world, the magical world where children live naturally, away from the ticking clock. The centre of our being exists beyond linear time, in a beautiful and limitless world where everything flows naturally.

A good exercise is to pick a day when you are free of obligations. Put away all clocks the night before, and forget about time. Wake up when you are ready. Your body will tell you when it is hungry, and the Sun will tell you when evening is near. Free yourself from television, radio and computers, and relax into a timeless world where you will start to feel the rhythms of your body and your own natural pace of living.

Even if you can't live your life this way all the time, it is a lovely place to go when you need some peace and calm.

It's simple really…

# Quintessence

> *Physics is the immortal Soul using its brain.*
> Professor Robert Pope

The feminine spirit has now appeared in the world of science, where cosmologists are searching for a mysterious substance that they know exists in the universe, called dark energy. If proven, their theory will change the way we look at the universe. Dark energy is not dark at all, but invisible to the human eye. It is the missing piece of the puzzle that explains how the universe works. In ancient Greece it was known as Quintessence.

The 20th century worldview was dominated by the second law of thermodynamics – the heat/death law that sees the universe expanding into cold space and dying.

This belief in a finite universe is now being challenged with the discovery of Quintessence, and indicates that our universe is Infinite. Quintessence is the force that balances and stops the universe from collapsing.

In philosophy, Quintessence is the fifth element, after air, earth, fire and water. The Greeks described it as a sublime and mysterious substance, unseen, yet existing everywhere. With the rise of the feminine in our culture today from her imprisoned past, comes her qualities including the mysterious fifth element, known for centuries but ignored until the present day.

For centuries science, religion and politics have been dominated by masculine values, and male controlled technology has taken us to the edge of disaster. Finding the truth of how the universe works will ensure our survival. In the $5^{th}$ century BC, Epicurus believed that the universe was infinite, with many populated worlds.

In ancient Chinese philosophy, the feminine Yin is seen as dark space and the masculine Yang is the creation/action within that space. Women instinctively know this as they possess within their body the endless space where all life begins – in the womb. Yin and Yang are present within all life. One cannot exist without the other, and each is contained within the other.

If a computer was programmed with feminine logic, we would have a balanced viewpoint. Professor Robert Pope tells us that 'feminine logic can be considered to obey the laws of fractal logic, which extends to infinity. In nano photography the flame of a candle shows tiny diamonds being formed. This is beyond the understanding of our present chemistry.'

Quintessence is the glue that holds the universe together…

## *The Soul speaks...*

Beneath your busy lives
is a coral reef of beauty and bliss.
Find your way.
I offer you a glass bottom boat.

## The music of the spheres

The eternal feminine spirit sings with the music of the spheres, and the heart replies with its own special harmony. The universe – that eternal jigsaw of all that is and will be – holds the music in her vast womb.

Have you heard the music of the cosmos? Only in silence can you hear its alluring rhythm. The desert holds the sound in its vast, warm horizons, and the forest touches the sound as it moves through the trees. Focusing on a single leaf will take you through to the silence that is so rare in the city. At first you may hear nothing, for the chattering mind is insistent on its thoughts. But with patience the sound will arise on a smooth wave of joy, bathing you in its peace.

Place your fingers over your ears to close out all sounds, and listen to the sound of your blood moving through your body. This is identical to the sound of Gaia as she orbits through space, for we are her children and her body is our body. Our blood is her blood.

The ancient people of the Goddess sang with the music of the spheres and danced to its rhythms. They may have seemed primitive by today's standards, but our ancestors were powerfully connected to nature. They built majestic megaliths like Stonehenge and the Ring of Brodgar to celebrate the cycles of life, while remaining aware of their place in a vast universe.

The old ways are returning as Gaia seeks balance on her shores. The music of the spheres can be heard once more, and the 'people of peace' are returning. They can be found in all walks of life. The Irish call them the Tuatha de Danann[7]. They move quietly and peacefully through the world and need no news headlines to announce their existence.

Look around.

They are sounding the harmony…

## *Spirit of the Earth...*

Every petal leads to the inner sanctum
Every wing a gateless gate
Between the worlds

In nature's temple
The drums beat to her pulse
Anima Loci
A place of Soul
Where the Gaia opens your eyes
To her wonders

We are voyagers here
Often unseen
Unnoticed
Reaching uncharted places
Walking trackless roads

But there is always hope
Straight ahead there is a brilliant light
Follow it...

*Part 5*

*Renewal...
healing ourselves...
and the Earth*

## We set sail in our little boat heading west

Our lives wash over the Sea of Passions, constantly moving in cycles of eternal change. We uncover wounds that we have carried forever, so that they may be tended to and healed. Many hearts dip and dive into this sea, bringing to the surface some beautiful treasures. We learn to breathe underwater while we search among the shells and stones for the Pearl of Beauty.

However, if we want to find peace, we must eventually cross over the restless sea. Imagine a life of pure joy, where nothing disturbs the silken lake. It may seem like a world away, but it is right there in front of you.

All you have to do – is want it.
Looking for the life you came here for
Begin your journey to the sacred shore of Being, within the temple of the heart. When change comes, the great oceanic sea that washes the emotions will move at high tide, forging Light into the world of matter.

Billowing waves on a full moon will begin to work through you, clearing, healing and shining a light on the path ahead; leading you to what will nourish you.

This is how the Soul reclaims her sacred space.

We are transformational beings on a journey to the heart, preparing you for the greater life – the life you came here for. Sisters and brothers alike have had to face the inner shadows, buffeted by wind and sea…

Sail on…

Find your way…

Find the life you came here for.

## *The Soul speaks*

I will take you beyond the body,
to your dancing and ageless spirit.

## *Honour the Mothers*

Without the stone and tree of home to enfold you, fragments of the heart can break away, like lost boats upon a foreign sea. The great Mother says, 'You are a daughter of the Mothers; you possess great dignity and native majesty. Stand upright with self respect and demonstrate your wisdom. Just be who you are, that's all. And don't relent - not in the face of lovers or children.'

As a child I was abducted by the tyrant god Hades, with many years spent wandering through his dark and sullen land. Now I have returned to the light of joyous being; no longer a child, but carrying the golden light within.

The greatest moment was returning to my beloved mother, whom I yearned for constantly but could not find. Sometimes I could hear her calling in the distance, and I cried out – but she could not hear me. One misty day she found me wandering the hills, and took me home to the green land of my birth.

Never lose your mother. She is your link to the ancestral line of women that you came from. There is a reason why you chose their bloodline and their history may guide you toward your own authentic life.

Remember that their blood is flowing through your veins.

Honour the Mothers…

## *The journey below...*

Beneath the tree roots an inner traveller can wander, down through the stream of ancient days, to the dwelling place of the ancestors, where all is real and nothing is hidden. This is the resting place for Souls as they await the call to new life; a place the Celts call Annwn and the Australian Aboriginals call Beralku. The Druids calls this process the Tuirgin, the circuit of births, where we appear and disappear in a timeless dance of existence.

I found myself in Annwn during a meditation. It was a rather colourless land, and all I could see was a forest of grey trees. The trees slowly began to move closer and I realised that they were our human ancestors. Perhaps this is why some ancient cultures believed that humans came from trees. There was nothing fearsome about them, and they moved silently with bodies grey as ash.

Many masks are worn on Earth, but in the root world they are not needed. You are naked on arrival, left only with the riches of your true Self. Yet this place was not lacking in mystery for the ancestors know the future. There is no colour, race or religion there, so division does not exist.

All the time we spend on Earth with our prejudices seems a waste of time when viewed from the root world. When humans arrive here they see the unity of all life forms. The ancestors know that the brotherhood of man is not an ideal, but an inherent part of human nature that we have lost along the way.

Those who have been tossed upon the waves of life, are at peace in the root world, where problems no longer exist and where they can bathe in the quiet waters of rest.

I could see an orange glow in the distance, which stood out from the grey world around me. As I walked closer to the glow the ancestors slowly moved in front of me to block my view. I was only a visitor and not permitted to see what was there.

The ancestors welcomed new voyagers as they arrived, and smiled as each voyager gasped at the sight of the treasure…

## *Walking the Aum*

Gaia has an exquisite labyrinth of pathways through her natural world that heals the bodymind. A quiet walk through her green world holds the best cure for all her creatures.

When you stand very still on Gaia's green lands, her powerful presence will calm you and hold you. Her energy will rise through your body in waves. Your body is her body. Your song is her song.

Find a quiet place to Be. A small patch of green will do, and as your body slows down, your thoughts and breathing will follow. Walk slowly and attune to her rhythms. When your heartbeat is slow and strong, your heart is then beating in time with the Earth and the cosmos.

Gaia has her own music. Her song is one of many within the vast concerto of the universe that gives rise to consciousness and movement.

Relax your jaw and leave your lips slightly open. Without moving your lips, make a quiet 'au' sound while very slowly closing your mouth. You are now sounding the Aum. Aum contains three sounds and these are the first three stages of consciousness. The full sounding of Aum leads to the fourth state of supreme consciousness.

Aum was the first sound ever uttered by a human being. As the mouth opens we hear 'au' and as the mouth closes we hear 'mm'. It is the first and last sound, and all sounds come from this source.

As we sound the Aum in our third dimensional space, we will find out way back to the light. Walking with Aum brings you to unity.

Aum means Truth and Being.

Aum is the sound of the Sun.

Aum means Yes.

All forces unite into One.

## *A golden age rising...*

We now follow the path through the Indian cycles of time as they repeat themselves in the eternal journey of unfolding Creation, and whose totality they call Brahma.

When Brahma exhales, all movement begins and the universe unfolds. When Brahma inhales, the universe is reabsorbed and once again there is stillness. Earthly time is divided into four Yugas, or Ages that cover thousands of years and equal one Mahayuga. As with all physical life, each Age passes with the gradual degeneration of forces, and the ageing process.

The first Age is the Satya (gold) Yuga, pure and untainted like all newly born life. This was the time of Atlantis, when goodness and purity bestowed long life and the ability to move through the dimensions with ease. The stories of the gradual destruction of Atlantis are based on the eventual misuse of the great power that was available in this Age, as the link with spirit slowly declined. Atlantis was an example of the beauty of our true spiritual home, as seen through earthly eyes. Everyone has an image they carry of Paradise, and this is perhaps an ancient memory of Atlantis, as the Satya Yuga was a time when humans could bring heaven down to Earth. Spirit does not die, but when wrapped in physical creation, everything is subject to the laws of Time.

Each cycle overlaps the next, and gradually the Treta (silver) Yuga arrived. In this Age, the Indian Rishis sat by the bank of the Saraswati river listening to the sounds of the manifesting universe. Great truths were revealed to them in the form of the Vedas, but nothing was written down at this time. Many people still had a natural attunement to spirit, but as time progressed the universal sounds grew dim within them.

The Dvapara (bronze) Yuga came next. Degeneration continued and the voice of spirit was heard by only a few. Many of the great megaliths like Stonehenge were built by those who could still attune to spirit. This was also the time of King Arthur and Camelot, when valour and courage kept goodness alive in the world. Populations grew, but connection to the universe dwindled as mankind moved deeper into materialism, with many losing their way. Great souls like Arthur were aware of this loss and began to search for wholeness and re-connection to God in the form of the search for the Holy Grail. Arthur's death ushered in the Kali Yuga.

The Kali (iron) Yuga is the last of the cycle, and is the darkest and shortest Age. The Kali they speak of is the male god of strife who represents the destructive side of the physical universe, and reminds us that all physical life must eventually die to give way to new life.

Degeneration has reached an all time low, and it is no surprise to find out that we are living in the Kali Yuga right now. It may be the darkest part of the journey, but it also precedes a new Mahayuga cycle and a new (Satya) Age of light. The waves of a golden age are already washing over our world and the light is slowly returning. There are ancient stories of gods and kings who are asleep or who wait to return again to the world when they are needed. King Arthur is said to be asleep beneath a hill in England, and Kalki is said to return at the end of the current materialistic Kali Yuga cycle. Most religions await a great avatar that will end the destruction of this Age.

The current fascination with Atlantis is a sign of the return of the Light. Hindu astrology tells us that the new Satya cycle will arrive when the Sun, Moon and Jupiter are together in the Pushya Nakshatra. This happens at the end of July, 2014.

There are often many tests for those who are on the journey Home. Consciousness points the way to the sacred shore.

We are already calling the Golden Age into being. Gaia's children are calling forth a new day.

## You are a living yantra...

The yantra is an ancient Indian design that explains the essence of the universe: that all existence is ruled by a single principle from which all life comes, and to which all life returns. This principle has many names – God, Oneness, the Absolute, Peace and Love. The yantra contains a central dot or symbol and all paths lead to and from that centre.

Within the design there is usually an image of a lotus flower, known as the flower of the Soul. It symbolizes the journey home to the sacred shore, from darkness to light, as the lotus grows from the muddy depths of a pond or stream, into a beautiful pristine blossom that remains pure and unaffected by its surroundings, just as the Soul is forever pure.

The word yantra means 'to hold' the energy within a structure or organism, which then becomes the dwelling place for the One power to manifest.

You are that! You are a living yantra, holding the power of the universe within you; all actors in the play of Oneness, with an eternal heritage. Cherish this precious life as you unfold the petals of awareness that open you into the Light.

*Part 6*

*The path leads back
to the hearth*

## Relax by the hearth

Come out of exile and find your way home to the fire of the hearth; a safe harbour for those who seek the comfort of the fireside. The hearth is a reminder of the grace of the Sun, with its power pulled down through the heat of the flame.

The hearth has long been a welcoming symbol of safety and rest at the end of a day for all travellers on life's pathways. The starless road was familiar to many of our ancestors, who often travelled alone with no light to guide them. Today we have abundant light, but sadly the hearth is a rare sight into today's world.

Our ancestors built circular homes with the hearth in the centre of the room. The keeper of the hearth was usually a woman, and harmony was created as she kindled the masculine power of the flame. The Greeks called her Hestia, the living flame at Delphi – the flame that never dies. Lighting a candle brings you into communion with the magical elements that move the universe. The flame of hope burns eternally for mankind, and life is easier today than it was for our ancestors. So come out of exile and find the living flame in your life. Build a bonfire!

Home is where the Heart-h is.

## The call of home

By the fence at the end of the garden there is a sheer drop. I am high above Tobermory, on the Scottish island of Mull, looking down upon the crisp cold winter town.

The stick trees are bare and covered with ice. Surrounding islands seem so near on this blue water, blue sky day, though there are clouds in the distance promising rain.

All this beauty…the mountains…everything, will one day vanish back to the crazy universe, for we are all petals of a great unfolding cosmic flower. But for now old Alba looks majestic and proud as she stands in her frozen beauty. Her songs and mysteries wrap me in the warm blanket of her proud history.

When the heart sounds the call, it is time to touch the shores of home.

A piper on a distant hill is playing a sad lament, stirring the landscape into a swirl of mist and longing. The song of the bagpipes is the sound of the Soul as it moves through the people in the land of my birth.

It feels like the summit of Ben Nevis up here as I look out on distant lands, and I am sure I can see the coast of Ireland. The smell of sweet moist air lingers for hours in this ancient land of the Cruithne[8], with its bobbing boats and brightly painted buildings.

The little bush in the garden still has its leaves; a strange sight among the shivering naked trees. The flowers are quietly stirring and await the glory of springtime.

The wind whistles a familiar song of childhood memories, while the new life of spring slowly unfolds.

## *The magical island...*

The ferry moved silently toward Iona's shores. We were sailing through dense fog that appeared quite suddenly within minutes of boarding the ferry. The day was sunny with clear blue skies, and the little Scottish Isle could be seen in the distance from the shores of Mull. Then the fog arrived, wrapping us carefully in its soft white cloak, as if to protect us on our journey to the island known as the Mecca of the Celts. Was this the legendary Druid mist of protection? We were certainly invisible as we lapped our way across the Sound. The sea kissed the ferry with gentle waves, and it felt as if we were sailing in a large bath rather than the open water with Atlantic breezes. How appropriate to be swathed in mist as we sailed to the ancient Isle of the Druids. There was a beautiful silence on the ferry as if a state of grace had descended upon us, holding us in its stillness. The magic of Iona was already tangible.

Iona only became visible when the ferry docked at the jetty, and we could see the vague outline of buildings on the main street. The short walk to the hotel felt surreal as we moved through the eerie mist. But once inside, the smell of cooking and a warm fireside brought us back down to earth again.

Many visit Iona to retrace the journey of St Columba, who arrived there from Ireland in 563AD, bringing Christianity with him. They called him the Dove, and it was here that his monks produced the beautiful *Book of Kells*. Others come to walk the shorelines and visit the ancient ruins.

Some of the rock formations on Iona are said to be around 1500 million years old, making it one of the oldest places on Earth.

It is said that Iona is protected by angels, sometimes seen on the hills and windy grasslands. One day as I sat watching the waves lap onto her pure white sands, I could feel the pull that Iona had on life's weary souls, gently washing them onto her sacred shore of rest. As I walked along her shoreline, the world of consumerism and city life drifted away. Spirituality can hardly survive in the cold wasteland of materialism.

St Columba lit his lamp of hope on Iona centuries ago, and the spiritual landscape grows brighter every day, with beacons of light slowly appearing across the world. This is the news that the media cannot see – the light that shines constantly; a light that is described by St Teresa of Avila as *'a light that knows no night and nothing ever disturbs it.'*

When you sit on Iona's sacred shore and listen, she will awaken you softly without intrusion. Her wings enfold all who visit her, opening the heart to pure Love.

Iona's lamp, like the eternal flame at Delphi, shines across the world like a guardian angel of hope and love.

An I mo Cridhe…

# Voyage of the heart

> *There is stone in me that knows stone.*
> Kathleen Raine

Born within the protective arms of Edinburgh castle, I hear the voices of stone upon stone, from a past that still calls out from ancient towers. The majestic fortress watches over his lands, with seven hills circling his domain in windswept harmony. The crowds rarely hear the song of stone and tree, nor visit the white swans in the loch on the hill. Beside the seat of Arthur there is a beautiful wilderness, where kings and heroes once sat contemplating the future of their beloved country.

Childhood hours were spent pursuing the more important things in life, like searching for four-leaf clovers or watching cloud shapes as they wandered by. Those days remain in the heart, kindly eclipsing the darker memories. There are many wounded hearts in the world, working hard to release dark shadows from their childhood. My own was just the right mix to create awakening.

Beloved land whose heart beats with mine, my love for you opened the gate to *all* love. Your eyes shine within mine, your lifeblood flows through my veins, and how blessed I am with the gift of you. The great love for home and hearth always opens the heart to the sacred shores of spiritual life.

I inhale the landscape and fortress walls as if to take its energy with me, to sustain me on distant shores. But my heart is forever roaming the hills and watching the graceful swans on Dunsapie loch, high above the city. Swans will only swim in peaceful surroundings, and their presence is always a sign that the sacred shore is near. Watch them glide and feel the gentle energy of Gaia.

My home is now Gondwanaland, a place of wide open spaces and deep red earth, so vastly different from Alba's shores. The voices of the Aboriginal Elders tell us, 'This land is my backbone. My land is mine only because I came in spirit from that land, and so did my ancestors of the same land. My land is my foundation.'[9]

Their words help me to understand the powerful link we have with the land of our birth, and my heart feels at home when I see their children sitting on the grass looking for four-leaf clovers.

## My heart's in the highlands...

In the spiritual highlands you can witness the journey of the Soul through eons of time. This beautiful landscape is as real as the Earth, but cannot be seen with human eyes. It takes another kind of seeing, that happens naturally when you stop the chattering mind. It is not easy to stop the mind jumping from thought to thought, but if you can practice this for a few minutes each day, you will benefit greatly from the peace that washes over you. It is not a state of stupor, but a quiet alertness that leads to the radiant joy of the Soul. A simple act like watching a candle flame can lead you there, but you must watch with all your attention on the flame. Each time you find yourself thinking, bring yourself back to the flame. At this moment, there is only the flame.

Behind the constant movement of life on Earth, is 'the peace that passeth all understanding.' In the spiritual highlands you realise that behind all living things is the face of the Creator/God. Everything opens...unfolds... becomes. Everything that exists is a vital part of the Creation... The poet sings...

> My heart's in the highlands, my heart is not here.
> My heart's in the highlands a-chasing the deer.
> A-chasing the wild deer and following the roe.
> My heart's in the highlands wherever I go.

## *The Soul speaks*

All existence blends and weaves
into a tapestry of Oneness.
Every part of your life is sacred.

## *There is always Light*

Even in a mud puddle there is the full
spectrum of light…
Exotic blues becoming forest greens…
Blending into pinks and violets…
Floating on the surface of water and
surrounding mud as if to say…
'It matters not, for all is Light…'

# Part 7

# ...And into the Light...

## The journey above

Visualise…

Travelling on an endless road that curves into the distance, with only an occasional glimmer of what lies ahead. In the distance is a city of Light; a flash on the horizon that encourages you to continue toward its sacred shore. On the journey you carry your bloodline with you – those ancient ones who hold the patterns of your existence. (I have visited their abode, and flown with great wings over desert terrain to watch the Templars of Light march by). Yet the white city beyond the hill is even more alluring than the flash of angels.

There is always Light! Sometimes we *are* the Light for others. All life on earth is a journey that leads back to our true Home. Can you see it in the distance?

As you walk along the endless road that curves into the distance, the city of Light, like a magnet, will pull you onward.

Who can know the truth of life, except to turn within to the great wisdom of the Soul, while paying attention to the inner song that curves toward the Light.

## Kingdom of Light

The Soul sings, *I am a dweller of the fifth kingdom where the Great Love resides. All kingdoms intertwine, and I am as close to you as a whisper. Such bliss awaits the seeker who finds me! I am only a breath away…*

The physical world is the third kingdom of duality where matter unfolds the great drama of movement and sound. Each time you feel love for another living creature, know that you are in my world, where beauty comes from loving others.

In dreamless sleep you bask in the peace of the higher worlds. This is the purpose of sleep – to give you the deep rest that comes from the kingdom of Light. You can experience this deep rest while you are awake, but the busy, moving bodymind often has difficulty keeping still.

Many people have attained this blissful peace, and all living beings have the ability to experience it. There is no need to 'overcome' your world, and need only to see through the illusion of separation and duality. What you think – you will become, so lift your thoughts to the highest good for yourself and for the world. Be gentle and honest with yourself and others. This is the way home to the sacred shore of peace, where the door is always open.

Love is the guide and protector.
Love felt – is felt in all kingdoms.
Love given – is always returned to you.
Love is the outcome of everything in the universe.
Love is the answer to all questions.
Love unlocks every door.

Do you realise that you also lead a golden life in the higher worlds?
Love is always there for you in Spirit.
Love is the fuel of the universe.

The Great Love encircles you at all times.

Open your heart to this great mystery.

## Merging with the Ocean

You come from the great ocean of Oneness, each one a drop in the eternal unfolding. When the bodymind dies it is not the end, for there is no end in the higher worlds. You become everything.

You are everything now.

In a world of joy and strife it is important to attune to the highest love possible, as the cycle of kali yuga can be difficult, though temporary. Can you see through the illusion of separateness? This is the quest of the seeker, and all paths lead home to the Oneness of all things. Imagine the universe like a giant jigsaw where we are all pieces of the puzzle; all vital parts of the design. As separate parts we move through this world searching for happiness, but together as one we display the most beautiful cosmic design.

So why does pain exist? The pain comes from the feeling of being split from the Source, and life on Earth is the journey back to wholeness and joy. Yet in truth you are never separate from the Source. Joy comes when you become conscious of your inclusion in the great design. Whether you save an empire or build a fence, you are a vital part of the design.

You are a drop within the ocean, and an ocean within a drop, pouring back and forth eternally.

## *The Soul speaks*

Everyone has a purpose in life.
To find it and manifest it
is your reason for being alive.

## *An infinite universe*

Grass is still
Trees are silent
Gaia is spinning through space
too fast to imagine

Walking slowly
through green woodland
The universe is Light
There is no darkness

Does the universe
expand and die?
Or do you live
in an infinite world?

Expand into coldness?
Or long waves of eternity?
Grass is still
Trees are silent…

Infinity…

## *Angels descend*

When you awaken to the joy of Soul contact, an angel descends upon you and crowns you with light. Her wings of comfort will wrap you with a peace that is rarely found in the city. Yet this peace can be found anywhere because it lies dormant within you, waiting for the moment of awareness… the moment of sunrise. When you withdraw from the rush of life for a few minutes, to sit quietly with inner stillness, you will feel refreshed by the pure waters that wash over you. Can you stop thinking? Let all thoughts go and feel ripples of bliss as they lap on your own sacred shore.

Many dismiss angels as fantasy, but they are one of the great truths that break through the darkness in the world; these archetypes of light are very real indeed. Mankind has an angelic destiny beyond these earthly shores.

Awakened ones shine with their own special light, like beacons of hope sailing upon Earth's stormy seas. Finding your way to the sacred shore is indeed a boon, and the love you find will bathe you in its pure waters.

The angel of light is the spiritual ancestor of us all, and the human race is one family sharing equal parts of one Truth. Soul awakening in you may not instantly change the world, but it will change the way you view life, as you begin to see through its illusion. This is how you bring heaven down to the Earth. Your real self is pure joy. Your true self is an angel.

## A most exquisite illusion

The spiritual path does not always end in solitude and contemplation. It may also take you out into the world to help your brothers and sisters on Gaia's shores. Some are happy in their cosy nests, but others are trapped in their life experiences.

Who would ask for suffering? Who would welcome pain into their lives? The path often leads through the battlefields of Becoming, but victory is yours when you stand in the clear light of truth, though maybe a little sad at the loss of the most exquisite illusion.

Moving on from the past, you face the universal Creation that brought you here. You unveil the truth of peace and bliss beyond physical death.

You are an eternal being.

The White Lotus says, *The Soul of mankind is immortal, and its future is the future of a thing whose growth and splendour has no limit.*[10]

And finally, there is the hope that when the body does expire, that 'death' really will look like Brad Pitt![11]

## *The Soul speaks...*

All existence blends and weaves
into a tapestry of Oneness.
Every part of your life is sacred.

## *Lightbearers*

Beacons of light on every shore,
Our shepherds of the new day,
Across the world they resound as one,
guiding us on paths of peace.
New worlds overlap the old,
in small wavelets that gradually reach the shore.

Think of the action of water contained in a bath.
The more water there is,
the faster the water flows when the plug is removed.
Speed is created from the weight of the water.

And so it is with our world.
With 6 billion people and rising,
Gaia's family is moving forward to its appointed destiny.

Lightbearers have existed throughout history.
They are the World Servers for peace.
An ancient lightbearer once said,
'Blessed are the meek for they shall inherit the Earth'

Nothing can stop the new day…

## *Masterpiece of beauty...*

Such beauty! Such design!
Galaxies of planets with deep orange sunsets.
Intricate patterns from leaf to cosmos.
Can you comprehend the power that unfolds this
perfect design?
For it is perfect in its beauty.

Beyond the vast expanse of the night sky is a great light.
It shines brighter than the Sun.
For those who struggle, the light is dim.
Journey to the sacred shore and end your struggle, for the
Soul is untouched and free.

The Creator has many names – Oneness, God/dess, Divine,
Love - the great maker of worlds and mysteries.
Oneness manifests as the phenomenal world,
then exhales and the adventure begins.
All life becomes what it can be.
Such power!
When reaching the peak of what it can be,
the Oneness inhales and the universe is reabsorbed.
Then the Oneness once again…exhales.

## *Path to Peace*

The true path to peace is within us all.
By developing our spiritual self.
By touching the deep spirit within,
we will awaken the global heart.
Think of the love that you feel for your family,
friends, children, pets.
Can you feel that love for the stranger,
the orphan, or for humankind?

When you come back to your Soul,
you help the world along
in a quiet, yet powerful way.
The Soul only knows joy,
so joy will be yours.
Now is the time.
Go Gently.

## *Cascades of love*

Beloved, I honour you in all beings.
You are behind the face of the ones I love.
You are behind all beings,
All beings are you.
I honour you in all life.
Their movement is your movement,
Their life is your life,
Their heart…your heart.

You, Beloved, are the Oneness, God/dess, Absolute
All that Is
My heart is your heart.
My joy is your joy.
My life is your life.

## *The eyes of the Divine*

Behind the power of the universe,
the One power is breathing life into its Creation.
This universe is one of many…
We belong to it all.
We move with it all.

There are those in whom the flame of joy
has been extinguished by the waters of emotion,
and feel they don't belong.
We all belong.
We all move as one.
Everything has meaning.
That is truth…

Come gather together on earthly shores
and bring the Great Love into your world.
Ignite the flame of belonging in whatever way you can.
Live and love your part of the Creation.
Consciousness is the sign that you are on your way home.
Unite in the great unfolding.
What else is there to do?

## *The Soul speaks...*

All hearts meet in invisible space.
Follow your heart.

## *A never-ending journey*

Having faith in the eternal Soul brings many treasures into your life. The nectar of Soul contact is sweeter than honey. Find time to be still…

A peaceful walk in nature helps the bodymind to rest.
The mind at rest is in its natural state. It is the stressful life in the city that is unnatural. Soul contact will lift you above the clouds of despair. All actions have consequences, so be mindful of what you say and do. Keep your heart open to the great love that fuels the universe. Have faith that there is an absolute power behind all things. The power says, *I am the Source behind all manifesting worlds. The drama of life is my play and you are the actors. My life unfolds in your journey of returning to Love; to the happy ending, the goal or the treasure.*

That power always loves you. You were born from that power; a child of the universe. All will be revealed to you in your peaceful state. It may not happen overnight, so be patient and trust the process of your unfolding sacredness.

Gentle swans glide over the lake.
Angels descend in the heart, filling the world with their love.
The journey through Gaia's land is a great adventure.
In the distance you can see the sacred shore.

You are sailing Home…

# *Pathways that lead to the sacred shore...*

## *Books*

Bailey, Alice. *Ponder on This.* Lucis Publishing. 1971

Bingen, Hildegard von. *Scivias.* 1152

Burns, Robert. *Kilmarnock Poetry Edition.* 1786

Campbell, Joseph. *The Power of Myth.* Anchor. 1991

Challoner, H.K. *Regents of the Seven Spheres.* TPH. 1966

Cleary, Thomas. *The Secret of the Golden Flower.* HarperCollins. 1991

Goethe, J.W.von. *Faust.* 1808

Greywolf. *Interview with a Yew Tree.* British Druid Order. 1998

Crombie, R. Ogilvie. *The Gentleman and the Faun.* Findhorn Press. 2001

Frankl, Viktor. *Man's Search for Meaning.* Touchstone Books. 1959

Hall, Judy. *The Crystal Bible.* Walking Stick Press. 2003

Hauck, Dennis. *The Emerald Tablet.* Penguin. 1999

Pope, Prof. Robert. Conversations. 2011

Raine, Kathleen. *Rock.* Penguin Modern Poets. 1970

Rumi, Jalal'uddin. *The Essential Rumi.* HarperCollins. 1996

Whitmont, Edward. *The Return of the Goddess.* Crossroad. 1982

# Music

Anugama. *Shamanic Dream.* Open Sky Music. 2000
Asha. *Celestine.* New World Music. 1996
Coxon, Robert. *The Silent Path.* RHC Productions. 1995
Deuter. *Hands of Light.* New Earth Records. 1998
Elgar, Edward. *Enigma Variations.* 1899
Enya. *Exile. EMI Music.* 1988
Mozart, Amadeus. *Symphony 41, Jupiter, finale.* 1788
Rosalind. *Nature Spirit.* Otherworld Music. 2004

# Websites

Alchemywebsite.com – the alchemical paintings of Adam McLean.
Findhorn.org – spiritual and educational community.
Headless.org – Douglas Harding's website
Isle-of-Iona.com – Iona community.
Masaru-emoto.net – water crystal studies.
Otherworldmusic.com – Author's website.
Science-art.com.au – Prof. Robert Pope.

# *Notes*

1. Broceliande is the ancient name of the forest of Paimpont in Brittany, France. Merlyn the wizard wandered these woods and his tomb is there.
2. The Chipko Movement re-emerged in 1974 when peasant women in India prevented the cutting down of local trees by hugging them to protect them from the local Forest Department, who were intent on clearing the land.
3. Yggdrasil is the world tree described in the Norse Poetic Edda from the 13th century. It is a giant Ash tree that spans the lower, middle and upper spiritual worlds.
4. Earthchild is the musical story of a journey through the Otherworld. See author's website.
5. Scottish artist Adam McLean has reproduced the ancient alchemical paintings from the 15th century.
6. The seven rays come from the theosophical writings of H.P. Blavatsky, and can be found in her book *The Secret Doctrine*.
7. The Tuatha de Danann are the Irish people of peace, and are said to return to the world at the end of an age. This is a universal story of hope, similar to the return of Christ or King Arthur.
8. Cruithne is the ancient name for the people of Scotland and Ireland.
9. These are the words of Galarrwuy Yunupingu, as part of the community guide to the *UN Declaration on the Rights of Indigenous Peoples*.
10. These words are from the *Three Great Truths* by Mabel Collins.
11. Brad Pitt plays the role of Death in the movie Meet *Joe Black*, 1998.

# *Acknowledgements*

Many thanks to:

Julian Stephens for his photograph of the Mud Maid at The Lost Gardens of Heligan, UK.

Blue Banana Graphics and Design for the cover design.

Martha Heeren for editing.

MBS Press for guiding me down the publishing path.

www.ingramcontent.com/pod-product-compliance
Lightning Source LLC
Chambersburg PA
CBHW021115080526
44587CB00010B/532